In the Rainforest

Howard Rice

Table of Contents

Emerald Tree Boa

Golden Lion Tamarin

A Warm, Wet World

Imagine air that is thick with warmth and wetness. Birds chirp and monkeys chatter. Long, leafy vines twist around trees. Colorful flowers look up and try to see the sun peeking through the branches of tall, green trees.

What is this place? It is a rainforest.

Liwi

What Are Rainforests?

Rainforests are like other forests because they are filled with trees and plants. But rainforests are different in one special way. They are very wet.

Most rainforests get a lot of rainfall. They are also warm most of the time. In this way, trees and plants stay colorful and healthy.

Rainforests like this are called **tropical** rainforests.

Tropical (TROP-i-cul) rainforests are sometimes called **jungles**.

Rainforests get about 90 inches of rain each year. That's about twice as tall as you!

Other rainforests are wet, too, but for more reasons than rainfall. They get a lot of water from fog and the moist air that comes from nearby oceans.

There are many more tropical rainforests than **temperate** (TEM-pə-rət) rainforests.

Rainforests like this are called **temperate** rainforests. They are not as warm as tropical rainforests, but they do not get very cold either.

Where Are They?

Tropical rainforests are found near Earth's **equator**.

The **equator** (e-KWAT-ər) is an imaginary line around the middle of Earth. It is halfway between the north and south poles.

The Tropic of Cancer

The Equator

The Tropic of Capricorn

Temperate rainforests are found near coasts. They are further north and south of the equator than tropical rainforests.

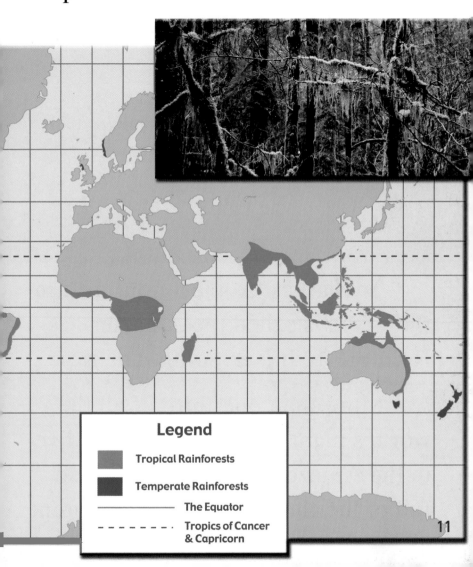

Legend

Tropical Rainforests

Temperate Rainforests

The Equator

Tropics of Cancer & Capricorn

Giant Sloth

Long Wing Butterfly Caterpillars

Jaguar

The largest tropical rainforest in the world is called the Amazon Rainforest. It is in South America.

More than one-third of all the world's plant and animal species live in the Amazon Rainforest! It is so full of life that about 50,000 different

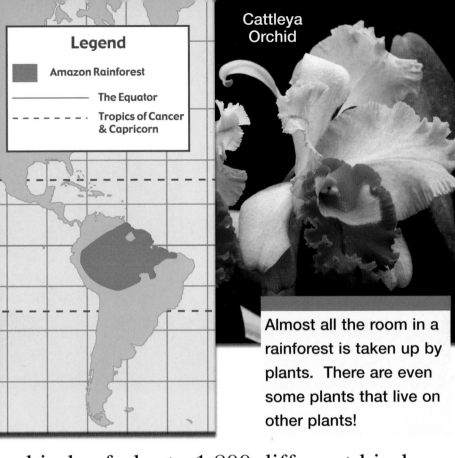

Cattleya Orchid

Legend

Amazon Rainforest

The Equator

Tropics of Cancer & Capricorn

Almost all the room in a rainforest is taken up by plants. There are even some plants that live on other plants!

kinds of plants, 1,800 different kinds of fish, and 1,200 different kinds of butterflies live there.

There are so many plants and animals in the Amazon Rainforest that we still do not know all those that live there.

13

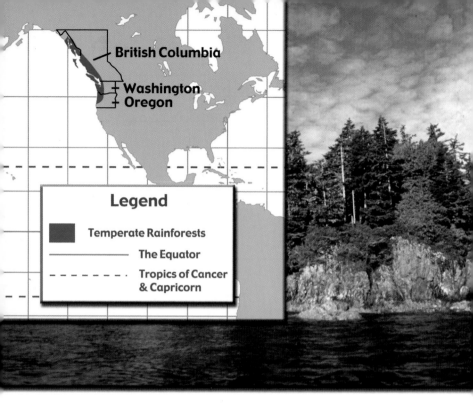

About one-fourth of the world's temperate rainforest is found in British Columbia in Canada. This rainforest is very old. Some trees have been living there for 2,000 years.

As old as this rainforest is, it is a baby compared to tropical rainforests. Tropical rainforests are millions of years old!

Trees keep growing all their lives. So, the oldest trees in this rainforest are very large. One spruce tree is 312 feet tall. One fir tree is 40 feet wide. That means that this fir tree is as wide as ten of your friends lying end-to-end on the ground!

Rainforest Layers

Tarantula

There are three layers of life in a rainforest. The first layer is called the **forest floor**. It is dark, wet, and soft. This is the area along the ground where many insects live.

Kiwi

Next comes the **understory**. It is cool and dark. Small trees and shrubs grow there. Butterflies and some small animals live in the understory.

Eyelash Viper

Finally, there is the **canopy**. This is the top of the rainforest's tall trees. Many birds and snakes live in the canopy.

Red-Tailed Parrots

Rainforest Animals

Black Bear

Raccoons

Animals of the temperate rainforest are mainly the same as animals you would find in the woods. Black bears, elk, beavers, and raccoons are just some of these.

Squash Bug

Red-Eyed Tree Frog

Half of all the animal kinds on Earth can be found in the world's rainforests.

Tropical rainforests are filled with jungle animals instead. There are monkeys, treefrogs, snakes, and jaguars there. Birds of all kinds and colors fill the trees. Insects as big as your fist buzz through the air!

Protecting the Rainforest

Even though rainforests are home to so many plants and animals, people of the world have been chopping them down for years. They use the land for farms and buildings. They use the trees for wood, paper, medicines, and more.

The most important thing we get from rainforests is the air we breathe. Plants and trees release oxygen. People can not live without the oxygen that trees and plants give them.

These things are important, but our rainforests are important, too. Many of our rainforests are gone forever. We need to protect the rainforests we have before it is too late.

Glossary

canopy

fog

forest floor

rainfall

temperate rainforest

tropical rainforest

understory